PAPER,
PAINT,
AND STUFF

A Calendar of Creative Art Ideas

Lois I. Myers

Karen B. Kurtz

More GOOD YEAR BOOKS® In General Methods and Centers

GOOD YEAR® EDUCATION SERIES
Theodore W. Hipple, Editor

ART CORNER
Bonnie Flint Striebel and
Ruth Beazell Forgan

**A CALENDAR OF HOME/SCHOOL
ACTIVITIES**
Jo Anne Patricia Brosnahan and
Barbara Walters Milne

**CHANGE FOR CHILDREN, Revised Edition
Ideas and Activities for
Individualized Learning**
Sandra Kaplan, Jo Ann Kaplan, Sheila
Madsen, and Bette Gould

**CREATIVE CONFLICT RESOLUTION
More Than 200 Activities for Keeping Peace
in the Classroom**
William J. Kreidler

**CURRICULUM PLANNING
The Dynamics of Theory and Practice**
Dale L. Brubaker

**DRUGS, KIDS, AND SCHOOLS
Practical Strategies for Educators and Other
Concerned Adults**
Diane Jane Tessler

**GAMES CHILDREN SHOULD PLAY
Sequential Lessons for Teaching
Communication Skills
Grades K-6**
Mary Cihak and Barbara Heron

GETTING THE MOST OUT OF TV
Dorothy Singer, Jerome Singer, and
Diana M. Zuckerman

**HANDBOOK FOR MIDDLE SCHOOL
TEACHING**
Paul George and Gordon Lawrence

**MASTERING THE MICRO
Using the Microcomputer in the Elementary
Classroom**
Dorothy H. Judd and Robert C. Judd

**ONE AT A TIME ALL AT ONCE
The Creative Teacher's Guide to
Individualized Instruction Without Anarchy**
Jack Blackburn and W. Conrad Powell

**THE OTHER SIDE OF THE REPORT CARD
A How-To-Do-It Program for Affective
Education**
Larry Chase

**PARTNERS
A Guide to Working with Schools for Parents
of Children with Special Instructional Needs**
David Lillie and Patricia Place

**A SONG IS A RAINBOW
Music, Movement, and Rhythm Instruments
in the Nursery School and Kindergarten**
Patty Zeitlin

**SPECIAL THINGS FOR SPECIAL DAYS
Holiday Ideas and Activities for Teaching
Children Ages 5-8**
Pat Short and Billee Davidson

**SURVIVAL KIT FOR TEACHERS
(AND PARENTS)**
Myrtle T. Collins and Dwane R. Collins

TEACHER'S BOOK OF LISTS
Sheila Madsen and Bette Gould

**TEACHER'S CHOICE
Ideas and Activities for
Teaching Basic Skills**
Sandra Kaplan, Sheila Madsen,
and Bette Gould

**TROUBLESHOOTING CLASSROOM
PROBLEMS**
Murray Tillman

**WHO'S TEACHING — WHO'S LEARNING?
Active Learning in Elementary Schools**
Dale L. Brubaker

**A YOUNG CHILD EXPERIENCES
Activities for Teaching and Learning**
Sandra Kaplan, Jo Ann Kaplan,
Sheila Madsen, and Bette Gould

For information about these or other GOOD YEAR BOOKS®, please write to
GOOD YEAR BOOKS®
Scott, Foresman and Company
1900 East Lake Avenue
Glenview, Illinois 60025

PAPER, PAINT, AND STUFF

A Calendar of Creative Art Ideas

**Karen B. Kurtz and Lois I. Myers
with photographs by Mark A. Kurtz**

Scott, Foresman and Company
Glenview, Illinois
Dallas, Texas   Oakland, New Jersey
Palo Alto, California   Tucker, Georgia
London

To Rachel Weybright and Rose Widmer,
friends and colleagues

Cover art by JoAnne Camacho; photograph by Mark A. Kurtz.

ISBN: 0-673-15989-2

123456—MAL—898887868584

Table of Contents

Preface

Paper, Paint, and Stuff is a collection of classroom art ideas for teachers of children in the elementary grades. The ideas are arranged by month to coincide with the typical school year, September through May. Within each month, the easier activities appear first with the more difficult ones following. An opening chapter, "Getting Started," encompasses our philosophy about and techniques for teaching art to young children. The concluding chapter, "Cleaning Up," covers terms, hints, and instructions to round out and complete the art experiences presented throughout the book.

We are grateful to the student artists whose creativity has been our inspiration, and we acknowledge the following students whose work is reproduced in this book: Melissa Alfrey, Pam Blackmer, Jamey Brock, Margie Broni, Ronda Bush, Hubert Camacho, JoAnne Camacho, Candy Clark, Beth Doane, Jerry Good, Matt Good, Mark Gross, Mike Groves, Jason Harvey, Britt Kaufmann, Jeff Kitson, Jason Letherman, Todd Method, Eric Miller, Stephanie Miller, Randy Neff, April Oligee, Troy Overholser, Thee Sonsaeng, and Dody Wayt.

Karen B. Kurtz

Lois I. Myers

Getting Started

Children are unique — bursting with freshness, creativity, and excitement. The teacher's joy is to listen to, observe, communicate with, stimulate, provide time and materials for, and join artists at work! The teacher invites children to become sensitive to their environment and experiences through:

Exploration. Say to your students: "Close your eyes. I have a surprise for you." Then brush each cheek with a silky soft pussy willow. Help the children explore pussy willows by asking them: "How did that feel? How do pussy willows grow? What colors tell us that these are pussy willows? How are they arranged on the stem? Where are the leaves? What shapes do you see? Could we show pussy willows on paper?"

You can also help the children explore with a piece of paper. Tell them, "Here is an unusually shaped piece of paper. How can we best use its space? Shall we add color? Lines? Shall we cut it? Could we bend or fold it? Try the best ideas!"

Observation. "We're going for a walk today to search for powdered gold, fly-away fluffs, and saw-toothed leaves! Dandelions — what bright little suns! What colors can we find? How many seeds are there on a puff ball? Blow one and watch the parachutes float! How could we use chalk to show dandelions?"

Or say to the children: "Choose a friend in this room. Observe your friend carefully. How are your friend's eyes spaced? How is the nose shaped? The mouth? What color is the hair? Does the person have any freckles? How is your friend feeling right now? Draw your friend's portrait."

Texture. Tell your students to close their eyes, and then distribute a smooth rock, a piece of fur, some sandpaper, or an open pine cone. Say to them, "Look at the pictures in your mind as you touch and feel. Describe what you are feeling. Does this object remind you of certain colors? What art tools could you use to help someone else know the feeling?

"You can make a rubbing by placing paper over an object and rubbing the paper with a crayon. Here is a thin piece of paper and a dark crayon. Look around the room. Find several surfaces that would make good rubbings. How many different rubbings can you make?"

Color. "What strange-colored things have you seen? A purple cow? Pink snow? Yellow water? How can these things be? What makes colors change? Can we make new colors by mixing paints?" Discuss light, shadow, and reflection with the children.

"What colors say, 'I'm so happy!'? What colors tell someone: 'I'm sad.' 'It's cold!' 'It's hot!'? How can we make a picture of a windy day? Can we show speed or slow and graceful movement?"

Sound. Tell the children to close their eyes. Read a poem and ask them, "How does this poem make you feel? Are there action words in the poem? What is happening? What might happen? How could we illustrate this poem?" The illustrations may be a single picture or a series of pictures.

Play a musical selection several times. Discuss the rhythm of the music. "How does the music make you feel? Do you see special colors in your mind at certain points in the music? How could we show loudness? Calmness? Marching? Use chalk on wet paper to make a picture or design that depicts the music."

* * * * * * * *

With all these exciting opportunities for being creative, who wants to fill in the spaces and stay inside the lines of ready-made patterns? As classroom teachers, we have found such patterns and duplicated pictures unfulfilling and confining. Children find the joy and freedom of their own self-expression both rewarding and satisfying.

Much of the success of each learning experience in *Paper, Paint, and Stuff* depends on your enthusiasm, confidence, and thoroughness in presenting the activities. Here are some ideas to help ensure the success of each project.

1. Be prepared. Work through the lesson yourself before presenting it to the children.
2. Have the necessary materials at hand.
3. Be explicit and precise as you demonstrate the lesson by working through the step-by-step procedures with the children.
4. Be sure the children understand what you are doing. It often helps to turn your back to the group when showing how to hold, fold, or cut.

5. Rejoice when you see individuality in the children's work. When they feel free to create for themselves, it means that you have given a superb presentation. We often tell our students, "We don't want to see *any* clowns (pictures, projects) that look just like ours. We can hardly wait to see *your* clowns!"

6. Ask questions that stimulate children's thinking and elicit their opinions about color, design, and form.

7. Provide some guidelines — e.g., an uneven number of objects is most exciting; use all the space; plan your picture before you begin; hold your project out at arm's length from time to time in order to check your progress.

* * * * * * * *

All the ideas in **Paper, Paint, and Stuff** have been successful with children in our classrooms. Some grew out of projects correlated with unit experiences, others from holiday celebrations; a few were developed as gifts the children could make and give, while many were designed for pure enjoyment. All reflect our daily contacts with children and colleagues — listening, learning, and discovering. We have found stimulation in a wide variety of sources: people, the environment, emotions, found objects, paper of all kinds, scraps, fabrics, things from home, throwaways, collectibles, nature walks, poems, music. . . .

We have shared with you our philosophy and some techniques to get you started successfully. You'll find that the projects are grouped by month to correspond with the months of the school year and that the projects become progressively more difficult. The final chapter, "Cleaning Up," offers hints, explanations, and instructions to round out the experiences presented throughout the book. For example, you'll find four specific suggestions (with directions) for matting and displaying the art your class creates.

Feel free to alter the ideas and experiment with the projects. Adapt them to your own best uses. **Paper, Paint, and Stuff** can serve as a springboard for fantastic originality and enjoyment. Be adventurous and have fun!

Most importantly, nurture creativity wherever you find it. And when you find it, allow it to blossom!

Vase

Each Student Needs:

    one 9x12-inch sheet of construction paper for the background

    one 5x6-inch sheet of construction paper for the vase

    dried weeds or flowers

    glue

    scissors

Procedure:

1. Fold the vase paper in half, matching the long edges.
2. Cut a vase or urn shape. Unfold.
3. Glue the side and bottom edges of the vase to the background.
4. Stick dried flowers or weeds in the vase.

Hands

Each Student Needs:

one 9x12-inch sheet of drawing paper　　　　crayons

Procedure:

1. Place a hand on the drawing paper, outline the hand shape with a dark crayon, and then lift the hand off the paper.

2. Repeat the hand outlines until the drawing paper is filled with hand shapes. The outlines should overlap.

3. Use other crayons to color in the spaces created by the hand shapes.

4. Color the background.

────── *VARIATION* ──────

Elephant

Each Student Needs:

one 4½x6-inch sheet of construction paper　　　　glue

crayons　　　　scissors

Procedure:

1. Place a hand in the center of the paper.

2. Outline the hand with a dark crayon.

3. Lift the hand and connect the outline shape across the palm.

4. Cut out the shape and turn it so that the fingers become the elephant's legs, the thumb becomes the trunk, and the palm becomes the body.

5. Add crayon accents for the ear, trunk, eye, and feet.

6. Cut a tail from construction paper scraps and glue in place.

Scribble Design

Each Student Needs:

one 12x18-inch sheet of drawing paper

crayons

Procedure:

1. Holding a dark crayon, close eyes and press the crayon firmly onto the surface of the paper. Scribble large shapes all over the paper.

2. Open eyes.

3. Choose other crayons to fill in or draw designs in the spaces created by the scribbling. Use colors that complement each other.

4. Color the background.

5. Mat and attach a title and the artist's name.

VARIATION

Find a realistic object in the scribble design, and then outline and develop the object. Color the background.

Looped Sculpture

Each Student Needs:

> assorted 1x12- or 2x12-inch strips of colored construction paper for the sculpture
>
> one 9x12-inch sheet of black construction paper for the base
>
> glue

Procedure:

1. Glue one end of a colored strip to the base.

2. Twist, twirl, bend, or curl the strip. Then glue it down.

3. Repeat steps 1 and 2 with the other colored strips.

4. Staple the sculptures to the bulletin board or place them in groups to decorate tables.

--- ■ *VARIATION* ■ ---

Cooperative Sculpture

Advance Teacher Preparation:

Staple sets of seven assorted 1½x18-inch construction paper strips at one end. Divide the students into groups of three to five, and give one set of stapled paper strips to each group.

The Group Needs:

one set of strips

stapler

yarn

paper punch

Procedure:

1. The children complete the sculpture cooperatively by twisting, curling, or bending the strips and stapling as needed. A strip may be stapled to itself or to other strips.

2. Continue until all the strips have been altered.

3. Hang the sculptures with yarn, either individually or stapled together into one large creation.

Name Design

Advance Teacher Preparation:

For each student, fold one 9x12-inch sheet of drawing paper in half, matching the long edges. Unfold and print or write the student's name on the fold line in dark crayon.

Each Student Needs:

folded drawing paper with name

crayons

rubbing object — pencil, scissors, ruler

Procedure:

1. Crayon over the name several times.

2. With the name on the inside, fold the paper on the line.

3. Rub the paper with a flat object. Unfold the paper when the negative design is formed.

4. Trace over the negative design with a dark crayon.

5. Look at the design created from the name. Color in the spaces. Color in the background.

6. Mat and attach a title and the artist's name. The **Name Design** can be adapted easily to pictures of monsters, bugs, or outer space creatures.

Chicken Little

Each Student Needs:

two wallpaper squares, one 4x4 inches for the head and the other 6x6 inches for the body

five or six 2x6-inch strips of construction paper for the tail feathers

one 2x6-inch strip of orange construction paper for the feet

glue

scissors

Procedure:

1. Cut rounded corners on the wallpaper squares to make them into circles.

2. Glue the head circle over the body circle.

3. Use construction paper scraps to add beak, eye, and comb.

4. Cut tail feathers from the paper strips. Glue behind the body section.

5. Fold the orange strip in half, matching the long edges. Draw a leg shape on the folded paper and cut out. This makes two legs. Glue the legs behind the body.

6. Glue the chicken to a background, place in a mural, or use as a border.

Turtle

Each Student Needs:

one 9x12-inch sheet of oaktag

scissors

glue

crayons

The Group Needs:

stapler

Procedure:

1. Use a dark crayon to draw an oval on the oaktag.
2. Use the dark crayon to mark grid lines on the oval to form the turtle's shell.
3. Color the shell.
4. Draw four large feet and a small tail in the corners of the oaktag. Draw one large head.
5. Color the turtle.
6. Cut all the pieces. Staple or glue the parts underneath the turtle's body.
7. To make the turtle stand, crease the legs and the center of the shell.

Clown

Each Student Needs:

    a 12x18-inch piece of fabric cut from a used, solid-colored bed sheet

    one 10x16-inch piece of cardboard backing

    one 9x12-inch sheet of oaktag

The Group Needs:

    iron   newspaper for covering work area

    masking tape

Procedure:

1. Cut rounded corners from the oaktag to form an oval face shape.

2. Place the face shape on the fabric and draw around the shape with a dark crayon. Remove the oaktag shape.

3. Use crayons to draw the clown's features and other details. Press heavily on the crayons to darken the color on the fabric.

4. Turn the clown facedown on the newspaper-covered work area, and with a warm iron press the underside of the clown thoroughly. The fabric will absorb the melted crayon.

5. Tape the clown to the cardboard backing.

6. Attach a title and the artist's name. Hang as a banner or stand upright.

Goldenrod

Advance Teacher Preparation:

Collect goldenrod.

Each Student Needs:

one 12x18-inch sheet of black construction paper

The Group Needs:

colored chalks

shallow pan of water

newspaper for covering work area

Procedure:

1. Dip the paper into the water *briefly*, enough to dampen all areas.
2. Lay the paper on the work area.
3. Select colored chalks and draw goldenrod on the damp paper. Cover the paper with goldenrod.
4. When the paper dries, mat and attach the artist's name.

───────────── *VARIATION* ─────────────

Dandelion

Advance Teacher Preparation:

Take the group on a walk to observe dandelions (leaves, blossoms, seed balls, roots).

Each Student Needs:

one 9x12-inch sheet of black construction paper

The Group Needs:

colored chalks

shallow pan of water

newspaper for covering work area

Procedure:

Follow the **Goldenrod** instructions, but fill the paper with dandelions.

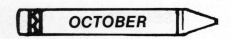

Leaves

Advance Teacher Preparation:

Take a group on a walk around the school neighborhood and collect leaves.

Each Student Needs:

one 12x18-inch sheet of drawing paper

leaves

crayons

Procedure:

1. Place a leaf on the sheet of drawing paper.
2. Use a crayon to draw around the leaf. Remove the leaf from the paper.
3. Repeat steps 1 and 2 until the paper is full of leaf shapes. The shapes may overlap.
4. Use crayons to color in the spaces and the background.

━━━ VARIATIONS ━━━

Crayon Resist

Each Student Needs:

one 12x18-inch sheet of drawing paper

crayons

The Group Needs:

brown tempera paint wash

brushes

newspaper for covering work area

Procedure:

1. Trace and color leaves as above.
2. Press crayons heavily onto the paper.
3. Apply tempera paint wash to complete the picture.
4. Dry.

Rubbing

Each Student Needs:

one 8½x11-inch sheet of typing paper

crayons

Procedure:

1. Place a leaf, vein-side up, underneath the typing paper.
2. Rub the paper lightly with a crayon.
3. Move the leaf to another part of the paper and repeat.
4. Continue until the paper is full of leaf rubbings.

Glue

Each Student Needs:

one 9x12-inch sheet of drawing paper

crayons

glue

Procedure:

1. Glue the leaf to the paper. Does the leaf resemble a real object?
2. Use crayons to develop the picture.
3. Mat and attach a title and the artist's name.

Ghost

Each Student Needs:

two white paper napkins

assorted construction paper scraps

scissors

glue

yarn

Procedure:

1. Crumple one napkin into a small ball.

2. Open the second napkin and place the crumpled ball in the middle.

3. Fold the open napkin around the ball, making sure that the ends hang free.

4. Tie yarn around the head of the ghost at the neck.

5. Glue construction paper features to the ghost's face.

6. Make deliciously scary mobiles with these ghosts — singly or in groups.

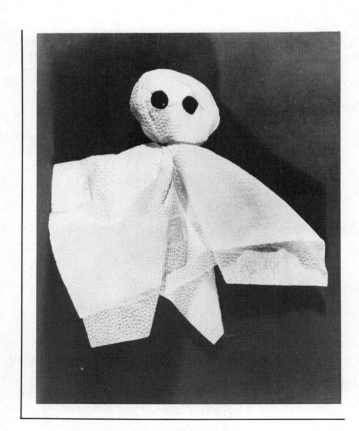

Columbus Day

Each Student Needs:

> one 9x12-inch sheet of gray or light blue construction paper for the background

> three squares of white construction paper — 2x2, 3x3, and 4x4 inches — for the sails

> three squares of assorted construction paper — 2x2, 3x3, and 4x4 inches — for the boats

> one 3x6-inch strip of blue construction paper for the waves

> glue

> scissors

Procedure:

1. Fold one white square in half to form a triangle. Crease for the sail. Repeat with the other two sails.

2. Fold a colored square in half to form a triangle. Crease and then unfold.

3. Fold the top and bottom tips of the folded colored square to the center of the fold line. Crease and then refold on the original fold line. This forms a boat. Repeat with the other two colored squares.

4. Discuss how the wind could blow sails. Match boats and sails by size. Place boats and sails on the background sheet and arrange to show perspective.

5. Cut the blue strip to make waves.

6. To create depth, glue only the boat and sail surfaces touching the background sheet.

7. Glue the strip of waves.

Tree

Each Student Needs:

    one 12x18-inch sheet of drawing paper

    brown crayon

The Group Needs:

    red, yellow, and brown tempera paint in small pans

    small squares of sponge

    newspaper for covering work area

Procedure:

1. Draw a tree trunk and branches on the drawing paper.

2. Dip the sponge squares in the tempera paint. Press the squares lightly on the tree.

3. Repeat with the other paint colors until the tree is full of colored leaves.

———————————— *VARIATIONS* ————————————

Winter Tree

Each Student Needs:

one 9x12-inch sheet of gray construction paper

black crayon

The Group Needs:

white tempera paint

sponge squares

newspaper for covering work area

Procedure:

Follow the **Tree** instructions, but fill the branches with snow rather than colored leaves.

Mural

Advance Teacher Preparation:

Have a sheet of paper large enough to cover the bulletin board.

The Group Needs:

tempera paint

brushes

newspaper for covering work area

Procedure:

1. Paint a tree trunk and branches on the paper.
2. Dip palm of hand into the tempera paint and press on the paper. This will make a large leaf shape.
3. Repeat until the tree is full of leaves.
4. When the mural is dry, attach it to the bulletin board.
5. The tree mural can be adapted to the seasons: an autumn tree with reds and golds, a winter tree covered with white, a spring tree filled with greens.

Hairy Head

Each Student Needs:

one 9x12-inch sheet of construction paper

assorted construction paper scraps, yarn, fabric, egg carton sections, buttons

glue

scissors

crayons

Procedure:

1. Cut rounded corners on the sheet of construction paper to form an oval face shape.

2. Cut and glue features from the assorted materials to develop **Hairy Head.**

Owl

Each Student Needs:

one 12x12-inch sheet of construction paper

assorted construction paper scraps

scissors   pencil

crayons   glue

Procedure:

1. Fold the construction paper square in half diagonally, crease, and then unfold.

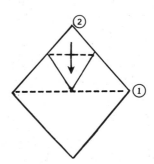

2. Fold the top corner of the square to the center fold line and crease. This makes a triangular flap for the head.

3. Cut away the triangle on each side of the head by cutting down from the top of the head to the center fold line and along the center fold line.

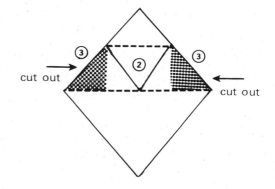

4. Cut eyes and a beak from the construction paper scraps and glue to the face.

5. Use a crayon to draw feathers on the body.

6. Cut fringe feathers on the bottom of the owl. Curl the fringe around a pencil.

Witch

Each Student Needs:

one 9x12-inch sheet of black construction paper for the body and arms

three 4½x6-inch sheets of construction paper — one black, one yellow, and one orange — for the hat, boots, accents, and head

glue

scissors

black crayon

Procedure:

1. Fold the body paper in half, matching the long edges.

2. Cut diagonally from the outer lower point to the upper centerfold. When unfolded, the paper will form a triangle. This becomes the witch's body. Save the scraps for making the arms.

3. Follow the same folding and cutting procedure with the 4½x6-inch sheet of black paper. This makes the hat. Save the scraps for making the boots.

4. Cut rounded corners from the orange paper to form a circle. This makes the head. Crayon curved lines to make the head look like a pumpkin.

5. Assemble all the parts and glue.

6. Complete the witch by adding yellow and black accents — broom, hands, facial features, hair.

Cat

Advance Teacher Preparation:

Cut one sheet of 9x12-inch black construction paper for each student in the following manner: two 1½x12-inch strips, two 6x6-inch squares (done by cutting the remainder of the sheet in half after cutting off the strips).

Each Student Needs:

black construction paper

one 4½x6-inch sheet of yellow construction paper for the accents

scissors

glue

Procedure:

1. Fold one black square in half, cut a heart shape for the body, and unfold.

2. Fold the second black square in half, cut a head shape with ears attached, and unfold.

3. Fold one of the strips into accordian pleats for the neck.

4. Fold the second strip in half, and cut on the fold line. Cut these pieces into the tail and feet.

5. Glue the parts together and add yellow accents — eyes, whiskers, nose, mouth, claws.

Scarecrow Collage

Each Student Needs:

one 12x18-inch sheet of construction paper for the background

one 4½x6-inch sheet of blue construction paper for the pants

one 4x9-inch sheet of construction paper for the shirt

one 3x3-inch square of flesh construction paper for the face

one 3x4-inch sheet of black construction paper for the hat

crayons

glue

scissors

The Group Needs:

straw or dried grass

construction paper scraps

fabric scraps for patches

Procedure:

1. Fold the blue construction paper and cut the pants. Unfold.

2. Fold and cut the shirt and the hat. Unfold.

3. Cut rounded corners from the flesh paper for the face. Add features with crayons or cut paper.

4. Assemble the scarecrow parts on the background sheet and glue in place. Add straw or dried grass for the hair, hands, and feet. Glue in place.

5. Cut patches from the fabric scraps to decorate the hat, pants, and shirt. Glue.

6. Make a stand for the scarecrow with construction paper or crayons. Add other accents — birds, garden plants, or trees — with crayons or construction paper.

7. Mat and attach a title and the artist's name.

Wild Thing

Each Student Needs:

one gallon milk carton   assorted construction paper scraps

newspaper   scissors

glue

The Group Needs:

tempera paint   newspaper for covering work area

brushes

Procedure:

1. Wrap the milk carton in two or three layers of newspaper. Glue the ends
    securely.

2. Paint the surface and then let it dry.

3. Decorate the carton with construction paper scraps formed into cones,
    curls, or strips. Egg carton sections, fabric, yarn, or cardboard may also
    be used.

4. Stack the creatures for a display.

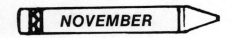

Change

Each Student Needs:

> one piece of yarn about 18 inches long
>
> one 9x12-inch sheet of construction paper
>
> glue
>
> crayons

Procedure:

1. Lay the yarn on the construction paper in an interesting pattern.
2. Glue the yarn to the construction paper.
3. Collect all papers and let them dry.
4. Redistribute the designs so that each child has the work of another.
5. Ask the children, "Does the design look like any real object you know?"
6. Develop with crayons. Color the background.
7. Mat and attach a title and the artist's name to each design.

━━━━━━ **VARIATIONS** ━━━━━━

   Prepare 9x12-inch sheets of construction paper by using either tempera paint or marking pen to add single black blobs or single black lines (curves, squiggles, angles) of varying size and position. The possibilities for completion of each design are endless.

   You may find it helpful to discuss the development of one or two designs with the group following redistribution of the papers. Such discussion often can stimulate their imaginations.

Fish

Each Student Needs:

one 12x18-inch sheet of construction paper

scissors

black crayon

Procedure:

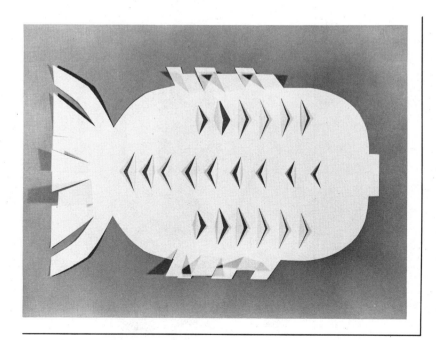

1. Fold the paper in half by matching the long edges.

2. With the fold in hand, cut an outline of a fish.

3. Keeping the paper folded, cut slits diagonally at intervals along the fold line. Slit the fins and tail.

4. Fold the fish in half again (matching the long edges) to create four thicknesses. Cut slits diagonally along the fold line.

5. Unfold.

6. Lift and with fingers crease the tail, fins, and slits.

7. Use the black crayon to color the eye.

————————————————— **VARIATION** —————————————————

Weave strips of construction paper through the fish's body.

Turkey

Each Student Needs:

one 9x12-inch sheet of white construction paper

crayons

Procedure:

1. Place a hand on the construction paper, and draw around the hand to create the turkey outline.

2. Lift the hand, and close the outline by connecting the two lines at the base of hand. The thumb is the turkey's head; the fingers are its tail feathers.

3. Use crayons to add feet, wattle, eye, and beak.

4. Using another crayon, draw around the turkey outline about ¼ to ½ inch from the first line.

5. Repeat until the paper is full of turkey outlines.

6. Color each area — turkey, outlines, and background — with crayon.

─────────── *VARIATIONS* ───────────

Collage

Each Student Needs:

one 9x12-inch sheet of oaktag

glue

scissors

The Group Needs:

an assortment of yarn, fabric scraps, pasta, buttons, glitter, seeds

Procedure:

1. Draw the turkey.
2. Use crayons to add the feet, wattle, eye, and beak.
3. Glue yarn, seeds, pasta, buttons, fabric scraps, or glitter to the turkey.

Torn Paper

Each Student Needs:

one 9x12-inch sheet of white construction paper for the background

one 4½x6-inch sheet of brown construction paper for the turkey

glue

crayons

Procedure:

1. Draw a turkey on the brown construction paper.
2. Use fingers to tear out the shape.
3. Glue the turkey to the center of the background.
4. Complete with crayons.

--- *VARIATIONS (cont.)* ---

Turkey on Fence

Each Student Needs:

three 4½x6-inch sheets of assorted construction paper for the turkey

one 12x18-inch sheet of construction paper for the background

glue

scissors

crayons

The Group Needs:

straw or dry grass

construction paper scraps

Procedure:

1. Draw a turkey on one sheet of the assorted construction paper and cut out.

2. On the remaining sheets, draw only the turkey's tail feathers (finger outline).

3. Connect the lines along the palm and cut out.

4. Arrange the feathers under the turkey. Glue.

5. Color the head.

6. Curl the tips of the tail feathers.

7. Create a fence on the background sheet with construction paper or crayons.

8. Position the turkey. Glue in place.

9. Add and glue cut-out pumpkins, crayoned bare trees, torn-paper leaves, and straw or dry grass corn shocks.

10. Complete with crayon accents.

Pilgrims and Indian

Each Student Needs:

> five 6x9-inch sheets of construction paper — two flesh for the Pilgrim faces, one brown for the Indian face, one black for the Pilgrim Man's hat, and one white for the Pilgrim Woman's hat

> one 2x3-inch piece of yellow construction paper for the hat buckle

> one 2x9-inch strip of construction paper for the feather

> crayons

> glue

> scissors

Procedure:

1. *Pilgrim Woman.* Cut rounded corners from one piece of flesh-colored paper to form the face shape. Add features — hair, eyes, nose, mouth, cheeks — with crayons. Glue white paper behind the head for a hat.

2. *Pilgrim Man.* Cut the face shape from flesh-colored paper and add features with crayons as above. Cut the hat from black paper and glue over the top of the head. Cut the hat buckle from yellow paper and glue in place.

3. *Indian.* Cut the face from brown paper and add features — eyes, nose, mouth, war paint, and headband — with crayons. Cut and fringe the feather. Glue the feather behind the head.

Blotto

Each Student Needs:

one 8½x11-inch sheet of duplicating paper

The Group Needs:

assorted tempera paint

brushes

newspaper for covering work area

Procedure:

1. Fold the paper in half and then unfold.
2. Place blobs of tempera paint on one inside half of the paper and along the crease.
3. Refold the paper. Press together and rub gently to transfer the blobs.
4. Unfold. Dry.
5. Mat or use as book covers.

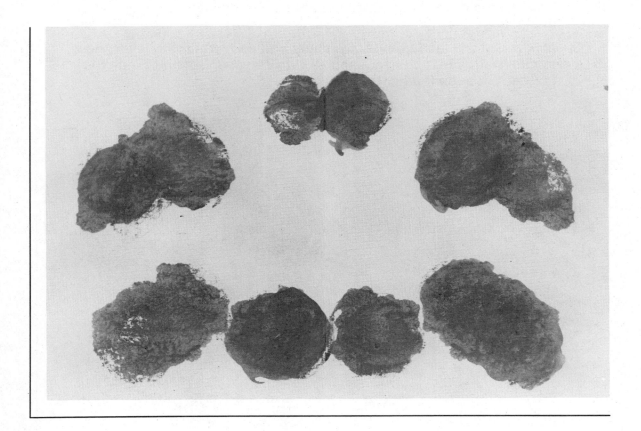

─────────── *VARIATIONS* ───────────

Cut Blotto

Each Student Needs:

one 8½x11-inch sheet of duplicating paper for the blotto

one 9x12-inch sheet of construction paper for the background

glue   crayons

scissors

The Group Needs:

assorted tempera paints   newspaper for covering work area

brushes

Procedure:

1. Make blotto as above and refold.
2. With fold in hand, cut objects (flower, tree) and paste them to the background sheet.
3. Develop and complete the picture with crayons.
4. Mat and attach a title and the artist's name.

Butterfly Blotto

Each Student Needs:

one 8½x11-inch sheet of duplicating paper for the blotto

one 9x12-inch sheet of black construction paper for the butterfly

The Group Needs:

assorted tempera paint   newspaper for covering work area

brushes

Procedure:

1. Make blotto as above.
2. Fold the black paper in half.
3. Holding the fold in hand, cut a butterfly shape.
4. Place blotto behind the black cut out.
5. Use black scraps to accent the butterfly body.

Melted Design

Each Student Needs:

one 4½x6-inch sheet of oaktag

The Group Needs:

old crayons

matches

candle

newspaper for covering work area

Procedure:

1. Hold a crayon briefly over a lighted candle.

2. When the wax gets soft, draw or drip abstract designs on the oaktag.

3. Repeat with other crayons until the oaktag is full of texture.

4. Mat and attach a title and the artist's name.

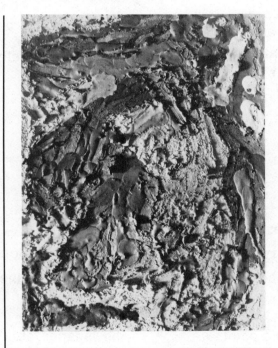

━━━━━━━━━━━ *VARIATIONS* ━━━━━━━━━━━

Calendar

Advance Teacher Preparation:

Purchase small calendar pads.

Each Student Needs:

    calendar pad

    one 3x4-inch sheet of oaktag

    one 6x9-inch sheet of oaktag

The Group Needs:

    old crayons

    candle

    matches

    newspaper for covering work area

Procedure:

1. Create a melted design on the 3x4-inch oaktag as above.
2. Mount the melted design and a calendar pad on the 6x9-inch oaktag. This decorated calendar makes an ideal gift.

Swab Painting

Advance Teacher Preparation:

    Bring in an electric skillet and small containers (baby food jars).

Each Student Needs:

    one 4½x6-inch sheet of oaktag

The Group Needs:

    old crayons

    cotton swabs

    newspaper for covering work area

Procedure:

1. Separate the crayons into like colors.
2. Place each group of like colors in a small container.
3. Place the containers in water in the skillet and heat.
4. Apply the melted wax to the oaktag with cotton swabs. Pictures may be realistic or abstract.
5. Mat and attach a title and the artist's name.

Fruit Bowl

Each Student Needs:

one 9x12-inch sheet of construction paper for the background

one 6x9-inch sheet of construction paper for the bowl

three 3x3-inch squares of construction paper — one orange, one yellow, one red — for the orange, pear, and apple

two 2½x6-inch pieces of construction paper — one purple and one yellow — for the grapes and banana

one 3½x4-inch piece of light green construction paper for the grapes

crayons

glue

scissors

Procedure:

1. Fold the bowl paper in half, matching the short edges.

2. Holding the fold in hand, cut half of the bowl shape. Unfold.

3. Cut rounded corners on the orange and red squares so that they resemble an orange and an apple.

4. Use crayons to add stems, rosy spots on the apple, and indentations on the orange.

5. Fold the yellow square in half and cut a pear shape from it. Unfold and use crayons to add stems and rosy spots.

6. Cut a banana from the yellow strip and add crayoned lines to make it more realistic.

7. Cut scalloped lines in the light green and purple paper to create grape clusters. Add crayon accents.

8. Assemble all the fruit and the bowl on the background paper and glue.

Gift Wrap

Each Student Needs:

two or three sheets of white tissue paper

two sheets of stiff paper toweling or scrap duplicating paper

The Group Needs:

red and green tempera paint

newspaper for covering work area

Procedure:

1. Lay more than one thickness of tissue paper on the work area. More than one thickness is required due to the paper's transparency and its inability to hold paint. Keep the sheets on top of each other.

2. Crumple each sheet of paper toweling or scrap duplicating paper separately.

3. Dip one crumpled sheet into red paint, and then use it to press lightly on the tissue paper.

4. Lift and press repeatedly until the tissue paper is full of prints.

5. Dip the remaining paper towel into green paint and repeat the process.

6. Use all the tissue paper sheets together to make one gift wrap.

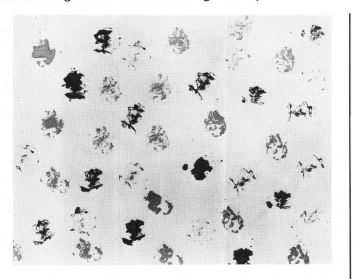

━━━━━━━━━━ *VARIATION* ━━━━━━━━━━

Follow the same procedure, but use sponges or other materials (combs, spools, feathers, cotton swabs) to print on the tissue paper.

Ornament

Each Student Needs:

    one canning jar lid, used but clean

    about 6 inches of yarn

    glue

    scissors

The Group Needs:

    used Christmas cards

    an assortment of glitter, lace, rickrack, or other trims

    hammer

    nail

Procedure:

1. Use the hammer and nail to punch a hole in the canning lid.

2. Thread the yarn through the hole and knot it.

3. Cut out Christmas scenes from the cards, and glue the scenes to the lid.

4. Trim the edge of the lid by gluing rickrack, glitter, or lace. Dry.

VARIATION

Make the ornament into a gift by gluing a student photograph to the lid.

Hidden Picture

Each Student Needs:

    one 9x12-inch sheet of drawing paper

    crayons

    scissors

Procedure:

1. Place the scissors in the center of the paper, and draw around the scissors with a dark crayon. Remove the scissors.

2. Ask the children, "Does the outline design resemble a real object?" Use other crayons to develop and complete the picture.

3. Mat and attach a title and the artist's name.

━━━━━━━━━━━━━ *VARIATION* ━━━━━━━━━━━━━

Follow the same procedure but alter the shape of the scissors — closed, partially open, fully open — before making the outline drawing. Or use different objects (coins, tape dispenser) instead of scissors.

Wrapped Ring

Each Student Needs:

    one plastic lid (from coffee, whipped topping, or soft margarine container)

    scissors

    glue

The Group Needs:

    yarn

Procedure:

1. Cut out and discard the inner portion of the lid, leaving a ring that measures about one inch in width.

2. Cut a piece of yarn about 24 to 36 inches in length.

3. Tie one end of the yarn to the lid, and then wrap the yarn around the lid. Glue in place.

4. Repeat steps 2 and 3 until the plastic ring is wrapped with yarn.

5. Cut off any excess yarn and glue ends together.

VARIATIONS

    Make two wrapped rings, both of equal size. Place one ring inside the other to form a sphere. Hang the sphere with yarn.

    Make two wrapped rings, one larger than the other. Suspend the smaller ring inside the larger one so that both turn freely. Actually, any smaller object — Christmas balls, pine cones, greenery, cut-paper snowflakes — may be suspended within the larger ring. Hang the concentric rings with yarn.

Same Color on Same Paper

Each Student Needs:

> one 9x12-inch sheet of construction paper
>
> crayons

The Group Needs:

> white tempera wash
>
> newspaper for covering work area

Procedure:

1. Choose a seasonal design — poinsettia, angel, candle, greenery.
2. Pressing heavily on a crayon, draw the design on construction paper of the same color as the crayon.
3. Paint the white tempera wash over the paper. Dry.

Santa

Each Student Needs:

one 6x9-inch sheet of red construction paper for the body

one 4½x6-inch sheet of red construction paper for the hat

two 3x4½-inch sheets of red construction paper for the mittens

one 6x7-inch sheet of white construction paper for the beard

one 2x12-inch sheet of white construction paper for the belt and trim

one 2x4½-inch sheet of pink construction paper for the face

two 3x4-inch sheets of black construction paper for the boots and trim

one 2x2-inch square of black construction paper for the buckle

cotton

glue

scissors

pencil

Procedure:

1. Fold the body paper in half, matching the short edges.

2. Holding the fold in hand, cut rounded corners on the bottom (open) edge. Unfold.

3. Fold the beard paper in half, matching the short edges.

4. Holding the fold in hand, cut scalloped curves along the three open edges. Keep the beard as large as possible. Unfold.

5. Fold the face paper in half, matching short edges.

6. Holding the fold in hand, cut two scallops on the opposite (open) edge. Unfold.

7. Fold the hat paper in half, matching short edges.

8. Holding the fold in hand, cut the hat. Unfold.

9. Use a pencil to draw a mitten shape on the mitten paper. Cut out and use as a shape for the other mitten.

10. Follow the mitten procedure to make the boots.

11. Using the black scraps, cut eyes, nose, mouth, and other features.

12. Shape, cut, and fit the belt to the body.

13. Using the scraps from the belt paper, cut trim for the mittens.

14. Cut the belt buckle.

15. Assemble all parts and glue in place.

16. Glue cotton to the hat for a tassel.

Looped Bird

Each Student Needs:

two 1x12-inch strips of construction paper for the body

one 1x6-inch strip of construction paper for the wings

scissors

pencil

The Group Needs:

stapler

string

Procedure:

1. Holding the two long strips together, cut the beak. Staple directly behind the beak.

2. Loop the top strip to form the head. Staple.

3. Loop the bottom strip to form the body. Staple.

4. Fringe the tail and then curl around a pencil, press, and release.

5. Place the shorter piece of construction paper across the back to form the wings. Staple.

6. Fringe the wings and curl them upward.

7. Attach string to the head and tail. Hang.

Stained Glass Window

Each Student Needs:

    one 9x12-inch sheet of black construction paper

    scissors

The Group Needs:

    colored tissue paper

    glue wash

    brushes

    newspaper for covering work area

Procedure:

1. Fold paper in half. Cut a tree shape. Unfold.
2. Tear tissue paper in strips.
3. Brush glue wash along the edges of the tree.
4. Press tissue paper strips onto the tree, covering the area. Dry.

Snow Scene

Each Student Needs:

    one 9x12-inch sheet of construction paper for the background

    crayons

    glue

The Group Needs:

    plastic packing material for snowflakes

Procedure:

1. Discuss horizon and perspective.
2. Use crayons to draw a snow scene on the background.
3. Glue snowflakes randomly to the picture.
4. Mat the picture and attach a title and the artist's name.

─────────── VARIATIONS ───────────

Torn Paper

Each Student Needs:

one 9x12-inch sheet of construction paper for the background

one 9x12-inch sheet of white construction paper for the snow

glue

Procedure:

1. Tear the white paper into pieces of varying shapes and sizes.
2. Assemble the pieces of white paper on the background to simulate snow, hills, trees, houses. Glue in place.
3. Mat the picture and attach a title and the artist's name.

Paint

Each Student Needs:

one 12x18-inch sheet of gray construction paper for the background

crayons

The Group Needs:

white tempera paint for the snow

brushes

Procedure:

1. Draw a snow scene on the background.
2. Use a black crayon to outline important areas (hills, trees, buildings).
3. Paint snow on hills, tree branches, and buildings. Dry.
4. Mat the picture and attach a title and the artist's name.

Snowflake

Each Student Needs:

    one 8x8-inch square of typing paper

    scissors

Procedure:

1. Fold the paper in half diagonally, forming a triangle. Crease the fold.

2. Pinch a small center mark in the middle of the fold line.

3. Using the small pinch mark as a guide, fold the triangle into three parts. Crease the folds.

4. Fold the triangle in half again. Crease the fold.

5. Cut diagonally to remove the top ends of the folded paper.

6. Cut diamonds, squares, hearts, and slits into the paper to create interesting patterns. Keep cutting until most of the paper is gone.

7. Unfold the paper gently.

━━━━━━━━━━━━━━━ *VARIATION* ━━━━━━━━━━━━━━━

Colored Snowflakes

Each Student Needs:

    one 9x12-inch sheet of white construction paper for the background

    three 5x5-inch squares of colored tissue paper for the snowflakes

    scissors

The Group Needs:

    glue wash

    brushes

    newspaper for covering work area

Procedure:

1. Cut three snowflakes.
2. Unfold and assemble on the background.
3. Brush glue wash over the paper.
4. Press each snowflake gently onto the paper. Dry.

Bird

Each Student Needs:

one 9x12-inch sheet of drawing paper

crayons

Procedure:

1. Draw an oval for the bird's body on the drawing paper.

2. Draw a circle for the head, and then connect the head and body with two lines for the neck.

3. Add tail feathers and wing.

4. Add feet, eye, beak, crest. Create different species of birds — cardinal, robin, bluejay — by adding appropriate characteristics and coloring.

5. Complete the picture by placing the bird in a nest, on the ground, on a tree branch, or eating a worm.

━━━━━━━━━ *VARIATION* ━━━━━━━━━

Flamboyant Bird

Each Student Needs:

    one large grocery bag for the bird

    two sheets of newspaper for stuffing

    glue

    scissors

    crayons

The Group Needs:

    stapler

    colored tissue paper

    construction paper scraps

Procedure:

1. Draw an outline of a bird on the flat grocery bag.
2. Cut along the outline, making sure that the cut goes through all thicknesses of the bag.
3. Staple along the outer edges of the bird shape.
4. Stuff the inside of the bird with crumpled newspaper.
5. Decorate the outside with construction paper scraps and colored tissue paper.
6. Punch a hole in the bird's head and hang.

Big Flowers

Each Student Needs:

    one 12x18-inch sheet of white construction paper for the background

    one 5x5-inch square of oaktag for the center of the flower

    crayons

    scissors

Procedure:

1. Cut rounded corners on the oaktag square.

2. Place the oaktag circle on the background, and then draw around the circle with a crayon.

3. Reposition the oaktag circle on the background and draw another outline around it. Repeat until the background has three or five flower centers. Then discard the oaktag circle.

4. Use other crayons to add petals, leaves, and stems to each flower.

5. Color the flowers, leaves, stems, and background.

6. Mat the picture and attach a title and the artist's name.

Winter Trees

Advance Teacher Preparation:

Take the group on a walk around the school neighborhood after a fresh snowfall. Notice the appearance of snow on trees, branches, and land. Discuss horizon and perspective.

Each Student Needs:

one 9x12-inch sheet of gray construction paper for the background

black crayon for land and trees

white chalk for snow

Procedure:

1. Draw land and trees on the background sheet.

2. Add chalk accents.

3. Mat and attach the artist's name.

Stitchery

Advance Teacher Preparation:

Thread yarn into needles. Tape each edge of mesh or burlap to prevent raveling.

Each Student Needs:

one sheet, about 12x18 inches, of mesh cut from a produce bag or burlap

scissors

The Group Needs:

needles

yarn

masking tape

Procedure:

1. Sew running, jumping, or walking stitches through holes in the mesh to create a design or picture.

2. Fill in.

3. Mat and attach a title and the artist's name.

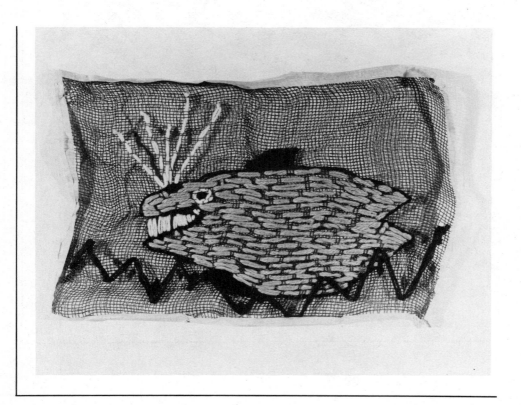

—————————— VARIATIONS ——————————

Fabric

Each Student Needs:

    one piece of fabric, about 12x18 inches, cut from a used, solid-colored bed sheet

    crayons

    scissors

The Group Needs:

needles

yarn

masking tape

iron

newspaper for covering work area

Procedure:

1. Draw a design on the fabric.
2. Place the design facedown on the working area.
3. Press the underside of the fabric thoroughly with a warm iron.
4. Stitch running, jumping, or walking stitches around the important areas of the design.
5. Mat and attach a title and the artist's name.

Egg Carton

Each Student Needs:

    one egg carton (bottom only)   scissors

The Group Needs:

needles   yarn

Procedure:

1. Stitch a design in each section of the egg carton.
2. Sew a yarn handle on top.
3. Hang.

Heart Design

Each Student Needs:

one 12x18-inch sheet of white construction paper for the background

one 4x4-inch oaktag square

crayons   scissors

The Group Needs:

red tempera paint wash   newspaper for covering work area

brushes

Procedure:

1. Fold the oaktag square in half and cut a heart shape. Unfold.

2. Lay the heart on construction paper, and draw around the heart with a red crayon. Press heavily.

3. Move the oaktag heart elsewhere on the construction paper, and draw another red outline. Repeat until the paper is full of heart designs. The shapes should overlap. Discard the oaktag heart.

4. Pressing heavily, color all the spaces with crayons to create a darker impression.

5. Paint the entire paper with red tempera paint wash. Dry.

6. Mat and attach the artist's name.

VARIATIONS

Cut the oaktag into other shapes. Christmas bells, spring flowers, and March shamrocks are appropriate for seasonal designs. Geometric shapes — triangles, circles, and squares — are always effective.

Vary the paint color. Use green for shamrocks or blue for flowers.

Mobile

Each Student Needs:

five or seven 6x6- or 4x4-inch
    squares of construction paper

one wire coat hanger

glue

scissors

The Group Needs:

yarn

paper punch

lace trims or paper doilies

construction paper scraps

Procedure:

1. Fold a sheet of construction paper in half and cut a heart shape. Unfold.

2. Decorate the heart on both sides with scraps of construction paper or lace trims.

3. Repeat with all hearts.

4. Punch a hole in the top of each heart. Thread yarn through the hole and tie securely.

5. Tie the hearts to each other and to the coat hanger, varying the lengths of yarn.

6. Balance and hang.

Axes and Cherries

Each Student Needs:

one 9x12-inch sheet of drawing paper for the background

crayons

Procedure:

1. Draw axes and cherries on the background sheet.
2. Color the drawing.
3. Mat and attach the artist's name.

━━━━━━━━━━━ *VARIATION* ━━━━━━━━━━━

Crayon Resist

Each Student Needs:

one 9x12-inch sheet of drawing paper for the background

crayons

The Group Needs:

light blue tempera paint wash   newspaper for covering work area

brushes

Procedure:

1. Draw and color as above, pressing the crayons heavily onto the paper.
2. Brush with tempera paint wash. Dry.

Card

Advance Teacher Preparation:

    Discuss letter writing with the group.

Each Student Needs:

    one 9x12-inch sheet of white construction paper for the background

    crayons   scissors

    glue   pencil

The Group Needs:

    construction paper scraps

Procedure:

1. Fold the construction paper in half, matching the short edges. Crease the fold.

2. Cut the heart shapes from construction paper scraps.

3. Assemble the heart shapes on the outside of the folded construction paper in a random fashion.

4. Glue the shapes in place.

5. Add crayon accents for leaves, stems, and vase.

6. Write a letter on the inside.

Cut Heart Design

Each Student Needs:

    one 8x8-inch square of typing paper

    one 9x9-inch square of red construction paper for the background

    scissors

    glue

Procedure:

1. Fold the typing paper in half and crease.

2. Fold it in half once again, matching the short edges. Crease the fold.

3. Again fold the paper in half, this time diagonally. Crease the fold.

4. Cut heart shapes from all edges of the paper.

5. Unfold gently.

6. Place the heart design on the background sheet and glue securely.

7. Mat and attach the artist's name.

Wire Sculpture

Advance Teacher Preparation:

Bring in separated, multistrand telephone cable cut into yard lengths and some cardboard or wood for the base.

Each Student Needs:

wire

cardboard or wood for the base

scissors

The Group Needs:

stapler

Procedure:

1. Plan the sculpture, selecting a subject and size.

2. Fold one strand of wire back and forth to form the skeleton of the subject. Attach all parts.

3. Use additional wire as needed. Continue to wrap, bend, or shape the wire to complete the sculpture. When possible, accent motion or action.

4. Staple the sculpture to the base.

5. Attach a title and the artist's name.

Heart Animal

Each Student Needs:

one 9x12-inch sheet of construction paper for the background

two 6x9-inch sheets of construction paper

crayons

glue

scissors

The Group Needs:

construction paper scraps

Procedure:

1. Choose an animal. Cut heart shapes for the body parts.

2. Assemble the heart shapes on the background to form a picture. Glue in place.

3. Use the paper scraps or crayons to add accents.

4. Attach a title and the artist's name to the picture.

VARIATION

Create a person instead of an animal from the heart-shaped body parts. Proceed as above.

Fan

Each Student Needs:

one 9x12-inch sheet of white drawing paper   crayons

The Group Needs:

stapler

Procedure:

1. Draw enough designs to fill the paper.
2. Fold the paper into accordian pleats from a long edge. Make each pleat about a half-inch wide.
3. Staple one end of the paper for a hand hold.
4. Open the fan.

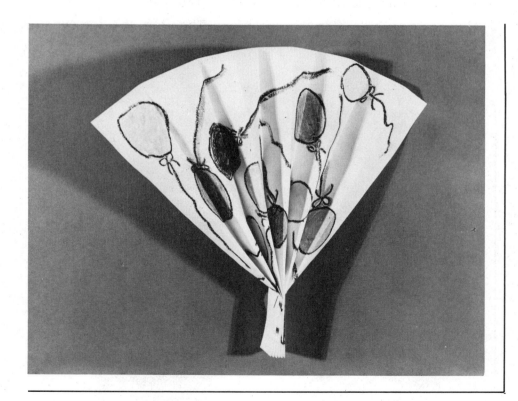

━━━━━━ *VARIATION* ━━━━━━

Proceed as above, but instead of drawing the designs with crayons, paint designs with tempera paint or watercolors and let dry.

Dog

Each Student Needs:

one 9x9-inch square of white drawing paper

crayons

scissors

Procedure:

1. Fold the paper in half diagonally and crease.

2. Pinch a small center mark in the middle of the fold line.

3. Lay thumb over the center pinch mark to create the top of the dog's head.

4. Fold the corners of the paper on either side of thumb to create the dog's ears. Make sure that the points of the ears extend beyond the head. Cut rounded corners on the tips of the ears.

5. Use crayons to develop the dog's face. Then turn the dog over, reverse the ears, and create another face on the other side.

Lamb

Each Student Needs:

one 6x9-inch sheet of white construction paper for the body

two 4½x6-inch sheets of white construction paper for the head and legs

one 4½x6-inch sheet of black construction paper for the features and hooves

strips of white construction paper for wool

glue

scissors

pencil

Procedure:

1. Cut rounded corners on the 6x9-inch body sheet.

2. Cut scalloped lines on one of the 4½x6-inch sheets for the head.

3. Glue the head to the top of the body.

4. Cut four legs from the other 4½x6-inch sheet. Glue the legs to the underside of the body.

5. Cut the features, hooves, and tail, and then glue in place.

6. Curl a white strip around a pencil. Press and release. Glue to the body. Repeat until the body is covered with wool. Younger children may need the strips (about 1x4½ inches) cut for them. Plastic packing material may be substituted for the paper strips.

Yarn Lion

Advance Teacher Preparation:

      Use a black marking pen to draw the outline of a lion face on sheets of 9x12-inch construction paper.

Each Student Needs:

    one 9x12-inch sheet of construction paper with lion face

    about 72 inches of yarn for the mane

    glue

    scissors

The Group Needs:

    construction paper scraps

Procedure:

1. Loop and glue the yarn around the face outline. More than the 72 inches of yarn may be needed.

2. Cut facial features — ears, eyes, nose, mouth, and whiskers — from construction paper and glue in place.

3. Attach the artist's name.

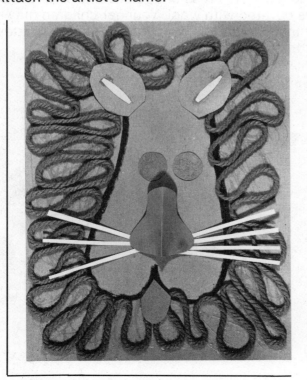

Paper Plate Lion

Each Student Needs:

one paper plate for the face

two 4x18-inch strips of orange construction paper for the mane

two 3x3-inch squares of white construction paper for the muzzle

two 3x3-inch squares of brown construction paper for the ears

scissors

glue

pencil

The Group Needs:

orange tempera paint   construction paper scraps

brushes   newspaper for covering work area

Procedure:

1. Paint the bottom of the paper plate and let dry.

2. Cut the mane fringe from the orange strips. Curl the strips around a pencil, press, and release. Overlap the strips and glue in place under the edge of the plate.

3. Cut rounded corners from the two squares for the muzzle. Glue in place.

4. Cut the ears from the two brown squares. Glue in place.

5. Cut the facial features from the construction paper scraps. Glue in place.

Shamrock

Advance Teacher Preparation:

Have scrap paper available so that students can practice making shamrocks.

Each Student Needs:

one 4x4-inch square of oaktag

one 6x9-inch sheet of green construction paper for the shamrock

one 9x12-inch sheet of white construction paper for the background

scissors

glue

pencil

Procedure:

1. Fold the oaktag square and cut a heart shape. Keep folded.

2. Place the folded heart on the long edge of the green paper, aligning the fold with the edge. Be sure to allow enough room to complete the shamrock.

3. Use a pencil to draw a line around the folded heart, and then remove the heart from the green construction paper.

4. Open the heart and put it back on the paper so that the point touches the edge of the paper and overlaps the drawn point of the folded heart.

5. Draw around the open heart with a pencil, and then remove and discard the oaktag heart.

6. Draw a stem.

7. Cut along the pencil lines. Keep both pieces to form a negative and a positive design.

8. Align the negative and positive pieces on the background sheet and glue in place.

9. Mat and attach the artist's name to the design.

VARIATIONS

Many interesting patterns can result from varying the size, number, and placement of the shamrocks.

Use the same procedure to create other objects — a tree, mushroom, flower, boat.

Kite

Each Student Needs:

one 12x18-inch sheet of construction paper for the kite

assorted 1x6-inch strips of construction paper for the tail

scissors

glue

The Group Needs:

shallow pan of water

colored chalks   newspaper for covering work area

Procedure:

1. Fold the 12x18-inch sheet in half, matching the long edges, and crease.

2. Beginning at the bottom of the fold line, cut diagonally to the midpoint of the open edge.

3. Beginning at the midpoint of the open edge, cut diagonally to the top of the fold line.

4. Unfold. The paper will form a kite shape.

5. *Briefly* dip the paper in water.

6. Decorate the wet paper with small chalk pictures, geometric shapes, or a design. Dry.

7. Glue the paper strips together to form a chain.

8. Glue the chain to the kite paper to form a tail for the kite.

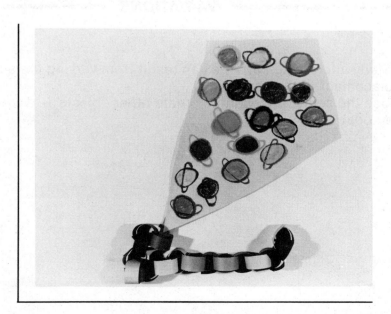

─────── **VARIATION** ───────

Tempera Prints

Each Student Needs:

> one 12x18-inch sheet of construction paper for the kite
>
> one 2x2-inch square of cardboard for the print
>
> scissors
>
> about 36 inches of string for the print

The Group Needs:

> tempera paint
>
> newspaper for covering work area

Procedure:

1. Repeat steps 1 through 4 of the **Kite** instructions.
2. Wrap all of the string around the cardboard square and tie securely.
3. Dip the square in paint.
4. Press the square firmly to print on the kite. Lift and repeat until the kite is full of printed designs. Use more paint as needed. Dry.
5. Attach a paper tail.

Plant

Each Student Needs:

one 9x12-inch sheet of white construction paper for the background

one 3x6-inch strip of green construction paper for the stem and leaves

one 6x9-inch sheet of colored tissue paper for the flower

crayons

scissors

glue

pencil

Procedure:

1. Cut the stem and leaves. Glue to the background.

2. Tear the tissue paper into small pieces. Wrap the pieces around the eraser end of a pencil, press, and remove.

3. Group the tissue paper pieces together to form a flower. Glue to stem.

4. Use crayons to draw the soil line, bulb, and roots of the plant.

5. Use a pencil to label parts: flower, leaf, stem, soil, bulb, root.

6. Mat and attach the artist's name.

Pussy Willow

Advance Teacher Preparation:

Collect pussy willows.

Each Student Needs:

one 9x12-inch sheet of gray construction paper for the background

crayons

The Group Needs:

white chalk

Procedure:

1. Draw pussy willow stems with brown crayon.
2. Draw pussy willows alternately on the stems with white chalk.
3. Outline the catkins with purple crayon. Add bracts with brown crayon.
4. Fill the sheet with pussy willows.
5. Mat and attach the artist's name.

Hanging Fish

Advance Teacher Preparation:

Draw a fish outline for each student on a 12x18-inch sheet of oaktag.

Each Student Needs:

oaktag sheet with fish outline	crayons
scissors	glue

The Group Needs:

assorted tissue paper scraps for scales	yarn
paper punch	

Procedure:

1. Use a black crayon to draw details — eye, head, scales, fins, tail — on the fish.
2. Color in the fish with other crayons. Choose colors that complement each other. Press heavily.
3. Turn the colored fish over and decorate the other side with details and color.
4. Tear the tissue paper into small pieces. Glue to the body for scales.
5. Punch a hole near the mouth of the fish and hang with a yarn loop.

Umbrellas

Each Student Needs:

one 12x18-inch sheet of gray or light blue construction paper for the background

one 4½x6-inch sheet of black construction paper for the handles

five or seven assorted 3x4½-inch sheets of gift wrap for the umbrellas

blue crayon

scissors

glue

The Group Needs:

clear plastic scraps

Procedure:

1. Fold a sheet of gift wrap in half, matching the short edges.

2. Cut an umbrella shape. Unfold.

3. Repeat steps 1 and 2 for all the sheets of gift wrap.

4. Assemble the umbrellas on the background sheet.

5. Cut umbrella handles and put on bottom of the umbrellas.

6. Cut umbrella points and put on top of the umbrellas.

7. Glue all umbrella parts in place.

8. Glue plastic scraps to resemble raindrops or draw in raindrops with the crayon.

9. Mat and attach the artist's name.

Egg

Each Student Needs:

> one 9x12-inch sheet of oaktag for the egg
>
> crayons
>
> newspaper for covering work area
>
> scissors

Procedure:

1. Cut rounded corners on the oaktag to form an egg shape.

2. Use a black crayon to outline a design on the egg.

3. Color the egg design, using a variety of crayons and pressing heavily.

=================== **VARIATIONS** ===================

Cracked Egg

Each Student Needs:

one 9x12-inch sheet of drawing paper for the egg

one 9x12-inch sheet of construction paper for the background

crayons

scissors

glue

Procedure:

1. Follow steps 1, 2, and 3 above to make the egg.
2. Cut the egg into large pieces.
3. Assemble the pieces in jigsaw-puzzle fashion on the background sheet.
4. Separate the pieces slightly and glue in place.

Egg Mobile

Each Student Needs:

one 9x12-inch sheet of oaktag

crayons

scissors

The Group Needs:

paper punch

yarn or string

Procedure:

1. Repeat steps 1 and 2 of the **Egg** instructions.
2. Design and crayon both sides.
3. Punch a hole in the egg near an edge.
4. Attach yarn or string and hang.

Bunny Puppet

Advance Teacher Preparation:

Collect small (7x14-inch) paper sacks. If the sizes differ from 7x14, adjust the other measurements accordingly.

If the group consists of younger children, staple the strips to create arm and leg springs (step 6) for them.

Each Student Needs:

one small 7x14-inch paper sack for the bunny

one 5½x7-inch sheet of wallpaper for the shirt

one 6x7-inch sheet of wallpaper for the pants

four 2½x2½-inch squares of black construction paper for the feet and hands

one 1x7-inch strip of black construction paper for the belt

two 2x6-inch strips of white construction paper for the ears

eight 1x12-inch strips of assorted construction paper for the arms and legs

scissors

glue

The Group Needs:

construction paper scraps   stapler

Procedure:

1. The bottom of the sack forms the bunny's head. The flap is the mouth and must remain free during construction.

2. Glue the shirt, pants, and belt papers to the sack.

3. Cut the belt buckle from construction paper scraps, and then glue in place.

4. Cut the ears and glue behind the head.

5. Cut and glue the bunny's features — eyes, nose, whiskers, mouth, ear accents.

6. To form an arm or leg, create springs by overlapping the ends of two strips at right angles, stapling, and then alternately overlapping the strips. Repeat the process with the other strips to form two arms and two legs.

7. Cut two hands and two feet.

8. Glue the hands and feet to the springs, and then staple the springs to the body.

Rabbit

Each Student Needs:

one 4x9-inch sheet of white construction paper for the body

one 3x4½-inch sheet of white construction paper for the head

three 1x4½-inch strips of white construction paper for the feet and tail

two 1x4-inch strips of white construction paper for the ears

glue

scissors

The Group Needs:

construction paper scraps for the features

stapler

Procedure:

1. Roll the body paper to form a tube. Glue or staple the ends.

2. Repeat step 1 for the head paper.

3. Glue or staple the head and body together.

4. Repeat step 1 for the feet and tail papers.

5. Glue or staple the two feet to the front of the body. Glue or staple the tail to the back of the body.

6. Cut the ears and other features. Glue in place.

7. Supported by its feet and tail, the rabbit will stand.

VARIATION

Follow the same procedure, but vary the shape of the ears and tail in order to create other animals.

String

Each Student Needs:

two 9x12-inch sheets of assorted construction paper

20 to 24 inches of string

one textbook

The Group Needs:

tempera paint

newspaper for covering work area

Procedure:

1. Immerse the string in tempera paint.

2. Lift the string from the paint and gently pull it between index finger and thumb to remove excess paint.

3. Place the string on a sheet of paper so that one end of the string extends over an edge.

4. Cover the string with the other sheet of paper. Align the corners of the two sheets.

5. Place the textbook over the paper and press firmly.

6. Pull the string out from between the two sheets of paper.

7. Separate the sheets and let them dry.

8. Mat the sheets or use them as booklet covers.

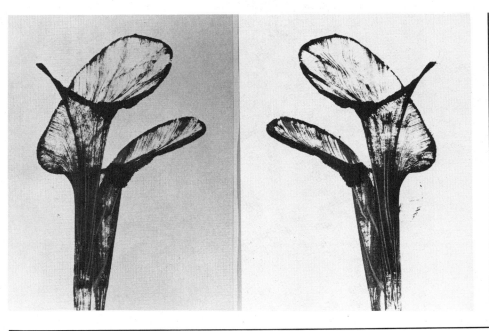

Sandpaper Rubbing

Advance Teacher Preparation:

Have an iron and medium-fine sandpaper available for this project.

Each Student Needs:

one 4½ x 5½-inch sheet of medium-fine sandpaper

one 4½ x 5½-inch sheet of white drawing paper

crayons

Procedure:

1. Draw a design or picture on the sandpaper. The picture must be crayoned heavily so that it will transfer.

2. Place the sandpaper picture facedown on the drawing paper.

3. Press with a hot iron until the design transfers.

4. Separate the sandpaper and drawing paper, mat, and attach a title and the artist's name.

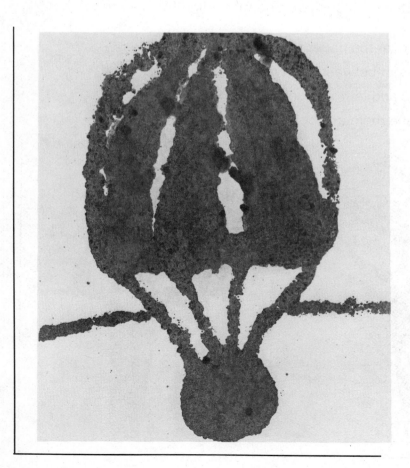

Tulips

Each Student Needs:

one 9x12-inch sheet of drawing paper   pencil

crayons

Procedure:

1. Fold the paper in half, matching the short edges, and crease.

2. Fold the paper in half again, matching the long edges, and crease.

3. Unfold the paper completely.

4. Fold the paper in half, matching long edges, and crease.

5. Fold the paper in half again, matching the long edges, and crease.

6. Unfold the paper completely. It will now be divided into sixteen rectangles.

7. Outline each rectangle lightly with a pencil.

8. Choose two crayons and use them to draw a tulip in one rectangle.

9. Plan a pattern or color repeat. Then draw a tulip in each rectangle. Press heavily on the crayons.

10. Crayon the background in a light color.

11. Outline each rectangle with black crayon.

12. Mat and attach the artist's name.

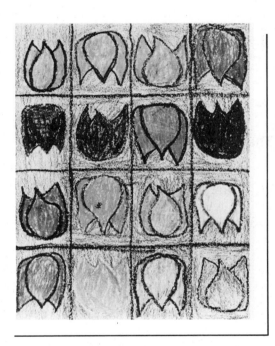

VARIATION

Proceed as above with another motif — mushroom, tree, animal, heart.

Bouquet

Advance Teacher Preparation:

Bring in the following materials: plastic hosiery eggs, buttons, pipe cleaners, Easter grass, and lace or rickrack scraps.

Each Student Needs:

three or five assorted egg carton sections for the flowers

three or five pipe cleaners for the stems

one plastic hosiery egg for the vase

modeling clay

glue

scissors

The Group Needs:

green tissue paper scraps for the leaves   buttons for the flower centers

Easter grass   lace or rickrack scraps

Procedure:

1. Invert the hosiery egg to make an hourglass shape. Anchor it in a small ball of clay to form the vase.

2. Glue lace or rickrack around the top of the vase.

3. Form another ball of clay and place it inside the vase.

4. Cut a flower from an egg carton section and insert the pipe cleaner stem.

5. Attach a button for the flower's center.

6. Repeat steps 4 and 5 for all the flowers.

7. Cut tissue paper leaves and glue them to the stems.

8. Secure the flower stems in the clay ball inside the vase. Arrange an interesting bouquet by varying the lengths of the stems.

9. Place the Easter grass over the clay.

───────────────── *VARIATION* ─────────────────

Chick in Egg

Advance Teacher Preparation:

Bring in the following materials: cotton balls, plastic hosiery eggs, Easter grass, and lace or rickrack scraps.

Each Student Needs:

one plastic hosiery egg for the vase

two cotton balls for the chick

modeling clay

scissors

glue

The Group Needs:

construction paper scraps for accents

Easter grass

lace or rickrack scraps

Procedure:

1. Repeat steps 1 and 2 of the **Bouquet** instructions.

2. Glue two cotton balls together.

3. Cut and glue construction paper accents for the eyes, beak, wings, legs, and feet.

4. Place Easter grass in the inverted hosiery egg and nestle the chick in the grass.

Cardboard Rubbing

Each Student Needs:

one 6x9-inch sheet of cardboard

one 9x12-inch sheet of cardboard for the background

one 8½x11-inch sheet of typing paper for the rubbing

glue

scissors

crayons

Procedure:

1. Cut a simple picture or design from the 6x9-inch cardboard and glue to background. Dry.

2. Lay the typing paper over the cardboard picture and hold securely.

3. Rub with the flat side of a crayon over the entire sheet of typing paper.

4. Choose another crayon, move the typing paper slightly, and repeat step 3.

5. Mat and attach the artist's name.

Watercolor

Each Student Needs:

one 9x12-inch sheet of white construction paper for the background

The Group Needs:

watercolors

shallow pan of water

two jars of water

black marking pens

newspaper for covering work area

Procedure:

1. Dip the paper into the pan of water *briefly*, enough to dampen the entire sheet.

2. Paint the damp paper with assorted watercolors, covering the total area. Be sure to keep the watercolors bright by washing brushes in one jar and picking up clean water from the second. Colors may run.

3. Dry the paper.

4. Use the marking pen to draw a picture that fills the page.

5. Mat and attach a title and the artist's name.

━━━━━━━━━━━ *VARIATION* ━━━━━━━━━━━

To make a greeting card, fold one 9x12-inch sheet of white construction paper in half, matching the long edges. Crease the fold. Repeat steps 1 through 3 above. Then draw a picture on the front cover only. Write a greeting or other message inside.

Geometric Puzzle

Advance Teacher Preparation:

Cut large shapes (rectangles, triangles, circles, squares) from 6x9-inch cardboard.

Each Student Needs:

one 9x12-inch sheet of black construction paper for the background

one 6x9-inch sheet of white construction paper

pencil

scissors

glue

Procedure:

1. Choose a cardboard shape and place it on the white paper.

2. Draw around the shape, cut it out, and discard the scraps.

3. Using curves, straight lines, and zigzags, cut the paper shape into large pieces.

4. Assemble the pieces on the background sheet in jigsaw-puzzle fashion, pull them apart slightly, and glue in place.

5. Mat and attach the artist's name.

━━━━━━━━━━ *VARIATION* ━━━━━━━━━━

Procedure:

1. Repeat steps 1 and 2.

2. Draw a large outline of a real object — tree, flower, animal — in the center of the paper shape.

3. Cut the object out of the shape.

4. Lay the object on the background sheet.

5. Cut the rest of the paper shape into large pieces.

6. Assemble the pieces around the shape in jigsaw-puzzle fashion.

7. Pull all the pieces apart slightly and glue in place.

8. Mat and attach the artist's name.

Daffodils

Advance Teacher Preparation:

Display actual daffodils.

Each Student Needs:

one 9x12-inch sheet of light-colored construction paper for the background

one 3x12-inch sheet of green construction paper for the leaves and stems

three or five 3½x3½-inch squares of yellow construction paper for the petals

three or five 2½x3½-inch sheets of yellow construction paper for the trumpets

crayons   pencil

scissors   glue

Procedure:

1. Fold one yellow square in half diagonally to form a triangle. Crease the fold.

2. Pinch a small center mark in the middle of the fold line.

3. Using the small pinch mark as a guide, fold the triangle into three parts. Crease the folds.

4. Cut a petal shape through all the thicknesses.

5. Unfold the paper, curl the petal tips around a pencil, press, and release.

6. Roll one trumpet sheet into a tube and glue together.

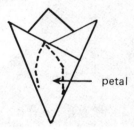

petal

7. Fringe one end of the trumpet and bend back.

8. Clip the other end of the trumpet, bend in, and glue it to the petals.

9. Complete all the flowers.

10. Cut stems and leaves, and assemble with the flowers on the background sheet. Glue in place.

11. Add crayon accents.

12. Mat and attach the artist's name.

─────────────── *VARIATION* ───────────────

Egg Carton Daffodils

Each Student Needs:

> one 9x12-inch sheet of light-colored construction paper for the background
>
> one 3x12-inch sheet of green construction paper for the leaves and stems
>
> nine 1x4-inch strips of yellow construction paper for the petals
>
> three yellow egg carton sections for the trumpets

crayons	pencil
scissors	glue

Procedure:

1. Fold one petal in half, matching the long edges. Crease the fold.

2. With fold in hand, cut rounded ends, beginning each cut at the fold line.

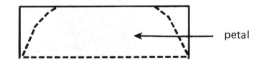

petal

3. Unfold the paper petal and repeat with two more strips.

4. Curl the petal tips around a pencil, press, and release.

5. Overlap three strips at their centers to form six petals. Glue.

6. Cut one egg carton trumpet. Fringe or scallop the top.

7. Glue the egg carton trumpet to the petals.

8. Complete all the flowers.

9. Repeat steps 10 through 12 of the **Daffodils** instructions.

Balloon Man

Each Student Needs:

    one 6x9-inch sheet of white construction paper for the picture

    one 9x12-inch sheet of white construction paper for the mat

    crayons

    scratching object — scissors, bobby pin, wood pick

    newspaper for covering work area

Procedure:

1. Choose several bright crayons, and then — pressing heavily — crayon wide bands of color over the entire sheet of paper.

2. Press heavily with a black crayon to cover all the colors completely.

3. Scratch a picture into the black surface, exposing the colored areas beneath.

4. Mat and attach a title and the artist's name.

VARIATION

Use the same technique to create illustrations for poems or stories.

Nature Mobile

Advance Teacher Preparation:

Take the group on a walk to observe a natural habitat (woodland, vacant lot, desert, pond, seashore) and help students collect inanimate specimens — nuts, small branches, tree bark, leaves, empty cocoons, skeletons, abandoned nests, rocks.

Each Student Needs:

nature specimens

one small (about 12-inch) branch

three, five, or seven assorted lengths of brown yarn

one piece of string (about 36 inches long) for hanging

Procedure:

1. Select three, five, or seven specimens.

2. Attach each specimen to a piece of yarn, and attach the yarn to the branch. Vary the lengths of yarn.

3. Attach the hanging string around the ends of a branch.

4. Balance and hang.

―――――――――――― *VARIATION* ――――――――――――

Nature Sculpture

Each Student Needs:

nature specimens   glue

one piece of wood or bark for the base

Procedure:

Assemble the specimens in an attractive arrangement, and then glue them to the base.

Pansy

Advance Teacher Preparation:

Display an actual pansy plant. Discuss the shape and color of the bloom and foliage.

Each Student Needs:

one 9x12-inch sheet of white drawing paper · · · · · · · · · · crayons

Procedure:

1. Choose two or three crayons of appropriate colors for each flower.
2. Use a dark crayon to draw five pansy petals.
3. Finish coloring the flower.
4. Draw three or five flowers.
5. Choose several shades of green to color the stems and foliage.
6. Color the background.
7. Mat and attach the artist's name.

━━━━━━━━━━ *VARIATION* ━━━━━━━━━━

Iris

Each Student Needs:

one 9x12-inch sheet of white drawing paper · · · · · · · · · · crayons

Procedure:

Proceed as above. The iris may be painted with a pale (yellow, blue, green) tempera wash.

Charcoal Sketch

Advance Teacher Preparation:

Choose a subject (picturesque building, trees, sculpture) or create a still life in the classroom (chairs, shoes, wheels).

Each Student Needs:

one 9x12- or 12x18-inch sheet of gray construction paper

one cardboard lapboard, about 20 inches square

one piece of charcoal

Procedure:

1. Practice with the charcoal and a piece of scrap paper to become familiar with charcoal sketching techniques.

2. Discuss horizon, perspective, shape, distance, size.

3. Sketch the subject.

4. Add accents.

5. Spray with fixative.

6. Mat and attach a title and the artist's name.

Cleaning Up

Cleaning up means more than washing away paint smears, displaying artwork, and storing supplies. This section sweeps together the loose ends. It clarifies terms and hints, emphasizes concepts, even suggests greater possibilities!

Here, in alphabetical order, are the main ideas we have covered throughout *Paper, Paint, and Stuff.*

Artist's Name: All children are artists! Give them the recognition they deserve by putting the word "Artist:" and the child's name on each piece of displayed artwork. Be sure to print or write neatly in a contrasting color.

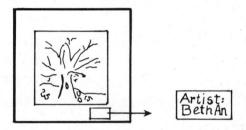

Artwork (Uses): Possibilities for utilizing children's artwork are limitless!

art fairs	illustrations for poems or stories
banners	mobiles
beautification	murals
booklet covers	placemats
borders	puppets
bulletin boards	sculptures
calendar covers	stationery
gifts for parents	stitchery
greeting cards	subject correlation for music, science, language arts
hall displays	table decorations
holiday decorations	wrapping papers

Charcoal (Drawing): Create different effects by varying the strokes and rubbing with a finger to shade.

Collage: A collage is a collection of various materials, flat or dimensional, glued to a background.

Collectibles: Consider sending a letter to parents asking for usable collectibles such as those listed below. Store until needed.

Collectibles	*Uses*
bed sheets (used, solid color)	stitchery, clowns
buttons	collages, eyes
cardboard (various weights)	lapboards, collages, rubbings, matting
coat hangers (wire)	mobiles

Collectibles	*Uses*
cotton (from medicine bottles)	hat tassels, tails, chicks
Easter grass	grass
egg cartons (colored plastic)	eyes, flowers, stems, stitchery
fabric	clothes, patches, kite tails
gift wrap (used or scrap)	umbrellas, chickens
hosiery eggs (plastic)	vases, eggs
jars (baby food)	painting, glue wash, storage
lace	collages, accents
lids (plastic or metal canning)	ornaments
milk cartons	sculpture, painting, storage
packing material (plastic)	snow, hair
pasta (uncooked)	collages, hair
pie pans (aluminum)	painting, storage
produce bags (mesh)	stitchery
rickrack	collages, accents
string	kite tails, prints, painting
telephone cable (colored, plastic-covered copper wire)	sculpture
wood scraps	sculpture base
yarn	stitchery, hair, mane, designs, mobiles

Corners: Room corners are great places to keep materials. Easy availability of materials encourages independent discovery. In a corner, place:

   a cardboard box filled with construction paper scraps

   crayons, clay, and drawing paper

   an easel with paper and chalk, crayons, or paint

   paste

   scissors

   writing paper

   yarn

Crayon Resist: Crayon resist is the process of crayoning heavily on paper, then brushing lightly and quickly with a tempera or watercolor wash. The crayon resists the paint. Larger brushes work better. Purchase several one-inch brushes for group use at the hardware store.

Evaluation (Group): Tour the classroom art gallery as a group and discuss each child's art. Encourage children to interact verbally and speak positively. Ask questions such as: "What does the picture express? How does the picture make you feel? What patterns do you observe? Do you see an example of perspective?" When children critique their own efforts and those of their peers, they learn to appreciate other artists' work — the photographer, the weaver, the oil painter, the potter, the florist.

Evaluation (Self): Enable children to evaluate their work critically. They should ask themselves: "Does this picture satisfy me? Have I used color well? Does any part disappear? Are the important things emphasized? Does anything need to be accented? Have I used space well?"

Facial proportion: Faces are generally oval in shape with the smaller end being the chin. To space features proportionally, place the eyes halfway between the top and the bottom of the oval. Place the nose halfway between the eyes and the bottom of the oval. Place the mouth halfway between the nose and the bottom of the oval. Develop and complete.

Fixative (Charcoal): Spray completed pictures with hairspray or a commercial fixative to prevent excessive smudging.

Gallery (Art): Make your classroom an art gallery! All efforts are acceptable and special, not only the ones you like best. Everything goes up for enjoyment.

Grouping: Pool teacher and student resources to minimize preparation time, provide idea exchange, and rotate responsibilities. Time is valuable. Here are some techniques for using time and space efficiently:

1. Group for "messy" activities (paints, chalks, washes) and when materials are limited (egg cartons, construction paper scraps, yarn).

2. Establish a group work area on the floor. Cover the area with plastic or newspapers.

3. Create a work area with a group of four to eight desks pushed together. Cover the surfaces with newspaper.

4. Set up a team area with an easel. Cover the floor with plastic. Students can use the easel with crayons and paper; chalk and colored construction paper; or sponges, paper, and tempera paint.

5. Establish separate work areas for each of the various steps of a single project. For example, students may select colored chalks in one area, draw goldenrod on a group of covered desk surfaces, and dry the completed pictures on the floor.

6. Capitalize on the fact that students learn from each other and are stimulated by each other.

7. Team teachers should divide responsibilities. For example, Teacher A guides the group discussion, Teacher B leads the learning activity, and Teacher C supervises.

8. The individual classroom teacher can use time efficiently by having groups doing different activities simultaneously. For example, one group of students can take turns at the work area(s) while the rest of the class engages in reading, writing, or mathematics.

9. Learning can be enhanced by new surroundings. Try the cafeteria for group writing, combine classes for outside hikes, utilize the library or any unoccupied area for other group activities.

Guidelines: These suggestions are intended to encourage children to experience the art mystique more completely and to observe more critically. When established early and taught consistently, these practices become second nature.

1. Utilize the total creative area by cutting, drawing, or painting to fill the space.

2. Keep the paper as large as possible when cutting round corners for circles or ovals.

3. The size of objects suggests their importance to the picture or to each other. Usually, more important objects are larger while less important ones are smaller. (See **Perspective**)

4. Visualize and plan. Say to students: "Close your eyes. Look at your picture in your mind. Think about and plan important objects, colors, and how you will use all of the space."

5. When definite objects (flowers, trees, balloons) dominate a picture, an uneven number of them is more exciting. Color, size, and random placement help move the viewer's eye.

6. Examine artwork periodically while creating. Hold at arm's length to check accents, balance, colors, important parts. Students should ask themselves: "Does this say what I want it to say?"

Horizon: The point at which the sky and earth appear to meet is called the horizon. Teach this concept by going outside to observe and discuss the horizon. Encourage children to establish a horizon and to place objects accordingly. Tell them: "People's feet walk on the earth. While tree tops may extend into the sky, their roots must grow in the soil."

Idea File (Teacher Resources): Establish a monthly file of art ideas. Include student art and bulletin board ideas.

Lapboard (Cardboard): Use lapboards when desk space is unavailable. To make lapboards, cut corrugated cardboard boxes in large pieces — approximately 20 inches square.

Mat (Picture Framing): Children react positively to neat and attractive displays of their artwork. Such displays nurture their self-image and reward them for their special efforts. Teachers, respect the creative gifts that children share with you.

Here are four ways to enhance and highlight student artwork.

1. For a 9x12-inch picture, cut a piece of cardboard approximately 10½x13½ inches for the back of the frame. Cut a piece of white mat board (available at a stationer's store) 11x14 inches for the front. To form the frame, cut an inner rectangle 7¾x10¼ inches from the mat board, leaving 2 inches at the bottom and 1½ inches on the sides and top. Turn both pieces facedown. Center the cardboard on the mat board frame which will extend beyond the cardboard on all sides. Fasten together at top and bottom with masking tape. Attach two reinforced fabric hangers and string to hang. Insert the picture at an open side, tacking — if necessary — to prevent sliding. You can later remove the artwork and use the frame again and again. You may substitute colored poster board or other types of cardboard for the white mat board.

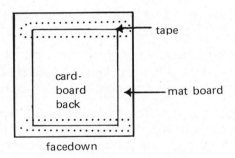

2. For a 12x18-inch picture, use cardboard approximately 14x21 inches for the back. Cut white mat board 15x22 inches for the front. Make the inner rectangle cut from the mat board 11x17½ inches, leaving 2½ inches at the bottom and 2 inches on the sides and top. Proceed as above.

3. Mount a 9x12-inch picture on 12x18-inch construction paper of a contrasting color. Be sure to write the artist's name and the picture title on the construction paper.

4. Spray an old picture frame with gold paint. Mat the inner portion with velvet. Attach the picture title and artist's name.

Mobiles: A wire coat hanger makes a bendable, pliable base for an individual mobile. A hula hoop suspended from the ceiling becomes the base for a group mobile. You can balance most mobiles by changing the position of the base.

Newspapers: Newspaper-covered desks or work areas simplify cleanup. Newspapers also protect surfaces when drying "messy" projects.

Painting (Sponge Squares): Cut one-inch squares from synthetic household sponges. Dip into paint and then print on paper. Wash, dry, and store for reuse.

Painting (Watercolor): Provide two jars of water. One jar is for washing all brushes. The second jar is for picking up clean water with brushes and adding to paint.

Paper (Dimension): Dimension adds excitement to artwork. To use paper dimensionally, students can create curls, cones, fringes, springs, loops, folds, pleats, and chains.

Paper (Utilization): Most projects in this book have been sized to utilize standard paper (8½x11, 9x12, and 12x18 inches) efficiently.

Paper (Fold Cutting): Teach children to hold the fold in one hand between the thumb and index finger. Cut along the open edges to prevent cutting on the wrong side and to avoid getting two half objects instead of one whole object.

Perspective: Perspective is the impression of distance. Teach this concept by placing an object of known size at a distance. While approaching the object, students should observe and discuss how varying distances make the object appear to change size. Encourage children to incorporate this concept in their artwork.

Positive and Negative Design: In a cut paper design, the positive is the part cut out. The remaining portion, or frame, is the negative. All pieces must be used.

Printing: Printing is the process of impressing a design or pattern onto a surface. The following materials can be used for making prints:

cardboard	plastic combs
cotton swabs	sponge squares
crumpled paper towels	string
feathers	wooden or plastic spools

Rubbing (Flat of Skinned Crayon): Peel crayon completely. Rub with the flat side of the crayon, not with the point. If possible, choose colors from the group crayon box.

Springs (Paper): Overlap ends of two strips of paper so that they create a right angle. Staple and then alternately overlap the strips back and forth over the staple. Glue or staple to base.

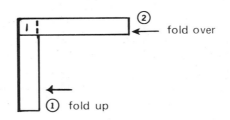

Stitchery: A variety of stitches creates texture and provides interest. For example:

Walking stitches (short even stitches on top and underneath)

Running stitches (long stitches on top, short stitches underneath)

Jumping stitches (long, angled stitches either close together or far apart)

Title: Encourage children to title some of their artwork. A title is a personal expression of the child's experience with the project. Include the title and artist's name on the matted piece. For neatness and legibility, the teacher may write the title for young children.

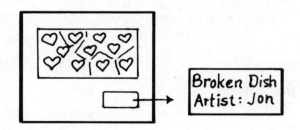

Wash (Glue): Use water to thin liquid white glue. Mix the two in a ratio of approximately one part glue to three parts water. Experiment before using as the consistency may vary.

Wash (Tempera Paint): Add two tablespoons of tempera paint to a pint of water. Experiment before using. Brush wash quickly and lightly onto paper. Do not scrub any area.

Wet Chalk: Wetting construction paper briefly before applying chalk will intensify the colors and act as a fixative.